How To Enjoy Interior Housepainting

A Primer To Get You Rolling

How To Enjoy Interior Housepainting

A Primer To Get You Rolling

Text and Working Illustrations by Richard Boesser
Cover and Historical Illustrations by Dan Drabek

Published by Richard Boesser • PO Box 8013 • Santa Cruz, Ca 95061-8013

Table of Contents

Natives the world over have used a naturally occurring form of tar to waterproof their boats. The Bible indicates that Noah used it, too.

Preface

This book describes all the steps, tools, and tricks-of-the-trade you will need to successfully prepare and paint any room in your house, from start to finish. It is the product of more than a decade of painting experience. During this time, I have had my own painting business, concentrating on private homes. I have learned first-hand what works the best, how to save time, and most important to homeowners, how to achieve beautiful, long-lasting results.

In this book I share all this experience with you. For years these steps and procedures have produced beautiful results and happy customers, and I still enjoy housepainting.

This book is arranged as an easy access handbook that you can quickly refer to again and again. The first part covers preparation in detail. Then, every aspect of brushing and rolling is discussed in depth.

Putting the steps together is easy, using the step-by-step quick reference guide that follows the main text. This lists the procedures to follow for every interior painting situation. A materials check list assures that you will have all the tools for a given job on hand, before you start.

Finally, sections on ladder safety, clean-up, stains and varnishes, paints, choosing colors, and even a bit of paint history make this the most complete guide to enjoying interior housepainting.

To break the ice, here are my definitions of a few terms that painters use: To "brush out" means to repeatedly stroke wet paint back and forth with a brush until it has uniformly covered a surface. To "cut-in" means to brush wet paint up to an edge where it meets a different surface or type of paint, and to leave that edge attractive and even. It also refers to applying paint with a brush in corners, prior to rolling. "Feathering" during preparation means smoothing out the rough edges of a defect and blending it into the surrounding area. During brushing, "feathering" is when you blend the brush strokes into one another to achieve an attractive, uniform coat.

For this book to be the most helpful, I suggest that you read a few sections each day, until you have finished the book. As you get ready to work, be sure to use the materials check list to confirm that you have everything you need before starting. Re-read the appropriate section right before you start working, and keep the book handy. When questions arise, refer to the table of contents, reference guide, or index. This way you will quickly find the answers that will keep you rolling along.

For their help, encouragement, and expertise, I would like to thank the following people: Helen and Bob, Bette and Bernie, Len and MJ, Dan and Nancy, Dick and Karen, Millie, Art, and Heather.

This book was written to present the techniques of interior housepainting that work for me. As the author/publisher, however, I shall have neither liability nor responsibility to any person or entity with respect to loss or damage caused or alleged to be caused directly or indirectly by the information contained in this book. So there.

Preparation

Through the years many of my customers knew that preparation is the most important part of the job. And it is. Fewer realized how long it takes to thoroughly prepare for the finish coat. In many cases you may spend three hours of prep for every hour spent applying the finish coat.

Preparing new work is very different from preparing existing work. New work includes raw wood trim, new drywall or plaster—anything newly installed that has yet to receive a finish of any kind. Existing work means re-painting something. There are fewer surprises in preparing new work, because existing work has a "history," with numerous layers of sometimes sloppy work. New work starts you off with a clean slate, yet both kinds can turn out perfectly with patience and care.

Simply put, proper interior preparation assures that your finish coat will a) stick a long time, b) be smooth and free of defects, c) dry evenly, and d) in some rooms, keep out moisture and splashed water from sinks, showers, etc. Complete preparation consists of scraping, sanding, filling, priming, caulking, and cleaning.

These six different operations are your paint preparation tool kit. Carried out in their proper order, they will give you perfect results that will stay beautiful for years. That's your goal, accomplished with careful use of the proper tools.

On the other side of the preparation equation are the surfaces you will encounter, and what the finish coat is going to be. Enamels, oil or acrylic, are the glossy paints that are washable. Oil-based enamels are the most durable. They can be applied to any surface inside the house that is to be painted, such as drywall, plaster, or wood. Flat latex, the less easily washed water-based wall paints, are usually confined to plaster or drywall use. These paints require different preparation steps. Also, the steps you use to prepare a new surface are different from those for an existing surface.

I will discuss each of the six steps of preparation, then list which you would use for each of the surface conditions that you will encounter. You'll be able to prepare any part of the inside of the house with confidence, knowing that the finished results will turn out beautifully.

Scraping

Scraping is not as big an issue indoors as out, yet will come up occasionally. In older, neglected homes it will come up a lot. Window sills often need a bit of scraping, due to the intrusion of moisture over the years.

A sharp scraper is an extremely useful tool once you realize that you control the bite by how hard you bear down. It is possible to scrape paper-thin layers with a scraper, or remove substantial amounts of wood. Blade sharpness and elbow grease determine how much. It does not require much pressure to remove loose paint in two or three strokes. Scraping is a balancing act between removing the loose paint and not damaging the wood. Following up with a light sanding, and then priming all exposed wood is the normal course to follow.

The scraper I use is the old-fashioned handle with interchangeable blades. There are at least six different shapes of blades. If you have elaborate trim to scrape, you may need many of them. Most situations call for only two basic ones.

Don't ever set one of these scrapers on the floor. Always place it on a counter or shelf close to a wall, so that you don't forget it's there and lean back on it when you are doing something else.

To sharpen your scraper, you will need a file that is suitable for filing metal. Ask at your hardware store. You will also need a scrap piece of 2x4, a foot or so long. This is to rest your scraper against as you sharpen, without dulling the blade.

With your file, stroke away from you along the edge of the scraper blade. At the end of the stroke, lift the file away from the blade and repeat. In other words, only stroke away from you when the file is in contact with the blade. Keep the file as even as you can with the angle that is already on the edge of the blade. Having felt the dullness before you began, notice how keen the edge becomes after 10 or 20 passes of the file. Rotate the scraper and repeat until your blade is sharp on all its edges.

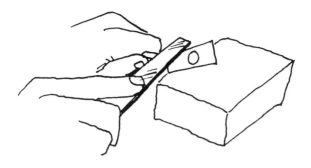

The round blades are a bit trickier, but the same process applies. You just have to make the pass around the curve with care, paying attention to keeping the angle of the blade as even as possible. As a final step you may wish to run the file flat across the other side of each edge once or twice, to remove the burr and increase the keenness of the edge.

When a scraper is sharp it makes a cutting noise, not a screech. If you have a good amount of scraping to do, sharpen your blade often. This reduces the fatigue that comes with struggling with a dull scraper. Also, with a smaller amount of elbow grease behind your strokes, the less likely you are to scar the wood when you slip. This happens no matter how careful you are, so don't worry. You will fill scratches along with the other surface defects later.

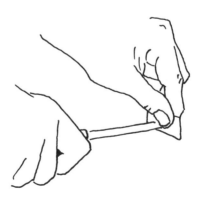

Scraping is easiest when you a) use only half the scraper blade and b) use a slightly angular pass as you stroke. Both these moves reduce resistance and allow the blade to do its job without skipping across the surface. Sharpen the blade frequently and take your time.

Scraping can also be done with a putty knife. Instead of the pull movement of the scraper, a putty knife removes loose paint with a push. This can be quite handy in tight corners where the scraper doesn't work as well.

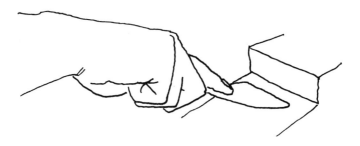

Scrape in the same direction as the grain of the wood at all times. If you must scrape across the grain in certain tight spots, do it gently. A sharp scraper will quickly deface raw wood when you pass it across the grain.

There may be some trim where you encounter a coat of paint that was applied to a poorly prepped surface. If, with a gentle pass of the scraper the paint pulls right off, you may wish to remove this coat. Your other option is to sand off the loose edges and glossy film, and then prime the entire section of trim, as mentioned in the sanding section. Just know that the layer of poor bonding is still there, only now buried under more paint. This kind of situation will chip very easily as long as that poorly bonded layer remains.

Decide how much time and energy you wish to spend in a situation like this. More moments spent now mean less maintenance in the future. Preparation has these trade-offs almost every step of the way. The more time spent in preparation always increases the life of the job.

Sanding

Preparing the wood trim takes the most time. Consider your standards, and how close to perfection you wish to get, before you start your sanding. At one end of the scale would be to remove the loose paint, sand the gloss off the trim paint, and put a fresh coat over that. The other end of the scale would be to work over every bit of trim and have it perfectly smooth everywhere, and then apply the paint. Your choice will depend on how much time you have, how important this kind of thing is to you, and how highly visible the spot is. After all, the inside of a hall closet isn't seen nearly as often as the window sill by the kitchen sink.

However, you should know that the difference in time between an average prep job and an excellent one is not that much. In many cases it may take only 20 minutes more per step to go over an area with extra patience that shows through so beautifully in the finished work.

I use a quarter sheet of sandpaper to work with. I don't wrap the paper around a block because a surface is seldom perfectly flat, and a block only hits the high spots. Dense-foam sanding blocks are available, which conform to dips and valleys a little better. So does the pad from a pole sander (more on this later), but I have enjoyed fine results using just my hand.

Little sanding machines can be a great help if you are sanding large amounts of smooth surfaces. Some sanders have two modes of operation: one orbital (circular), the other in-line (back and forth). However, machines are useless in corners, on window sash, complex trim, etc. They may save you time in some places, but they won't replace hand sanding altogether. Some broad, flat surfaces, like doors and cabinets, benefit most from power sanders or a sanding pad.

Sanding is an essential step in preparing to paint, and I will tell you the tricks I have learned. Always use a dust mask when you are sanding. Paint stores carry them.

Existing trim must be sanded before it can be re-painted. You must at least dull the gloss of the previous coat, so the coat you are applying will stick properly. Effort spent beyond this step depends on how smooth you wish that particular piece of trim. Sags from previous painters, brush marks from before, bits of dirt, all these are usually embedded in the trim of older houses. A new coat of paint will make things look cleaner, yet it will accent the blemishes you don't sand out, because the new coat will be shiny.

Grit #120 is perfect for dulling the gloss on wood trim. Sand the entire surface to be painted. Careful sanding will make your next coat grip tightly. Skimpy sanding won't hold paint as well over the years. If the entire surface has been sanded properly, the paint will grab better so that it is even and doesn't have thin, streaky spots. I have seen that rushing through the sanding process often means two finish coats, when one coat would have done it had I taken the time to sand every bit of wood carefully. A little bit more time spent sanding will make the final coat go on smoother and quicker, because you don't have to fuss with spots that are "showing through." The surface underneath grabs the paint readily after a thorough sanding.

The other aspect of sanding existing surfaces is when you run into peeling or chipped paint. You should sand smooth the edges of these areas so that the surface has an even look. This is called "feathering." Feathering does two things: it gets all the loose, flaky paint off, and it makes the sharp edges smoother. These are less noticeable after your finish coat has been applied.

Where wood is chipped away, you will want to feather the edges of the damaged area into the surrounding paint that is still gripping tightly. These spots will later be primed and filled, and are discussed in those sections.

If the existing top coat on your trim is latex, the job of feathering is tricky. Latex doesn't sand like oil-based paints. Imagine sanding a piece of plastic food wrap. Latex, after all, is a flexible plastic. Grit #120 is the grade of sandpaper that will work best on latex. Anything coarser scrapes away the latex in tiny lines and marks up the wood. If the coat of latex was applied to a poorly sanded surface, it will peel quite easily. Sanding an area back to a firm edge can be difficult because it wants to keep peeling. There are several solutions. You can scrape the entire coat off, which takes a lot of time and patience. You can also scrape it off only in those areas that are most noticeable—those things that are right at eye level—and leave the transition edge farther down.

I have found a very useful solution to this problem. Put a coat of primer over the entire surface once the gloss and any loose paint have been sanded down. The primer "locks down" the paint at these weak edges. When dry, gently sanding these edges works much better. A nice feathered edge can be obtained. Peeling is halted by the primer that has sealed around and under these edges.

Sanding oil-based paints is a much easier operation. If the existing top coat is oil, your feathering is a breeze and sanding works as it should. Again, use 120 grit and a dust mask. Remember that anything coarser than 120, that is, with a lower numbered grit, will show sanding marks through your finish coat. If you desire a mirror finish, follow up with a light sand using 150 grit.

The ancient Egyptians used natural minerals as pigments. These included red and yellow ochres, green earth, and charcoal. Using egg, lime, and gum arabic, or specially treated bees wax to hold the pigments together, they developed encaustic, a coating that was applied hot. This was the way to water-proof and preserve things in antiquity, while adding beauty at the same time.

I have always waited to sand new trim until after I have oil primed the raw wood. The reason is that as the oil penetrates the wood, it kicks up fibers. (It happens with latex primers too.) This is called "whiskering," an appropriate term. You then shave off these whiskers with the sandpaper. Sanding the prime coat also reduces brush marks. I have found that gently using 100 grit is very effective on rougher raw wood that has been oil primed. Sandpaper weakens as you use it, and it can cut and scratch surfaces when it is fresh. For this reason, go gently with the 100 at first. It will begin to dull, and in this state it is perfect for sanding oil-primed wood. Follow up with a gentle 120 grit sanding to remove scratches from the 100 grit.

To smooth moldings that have a complex surface profile, steel wool can be very useful. Where sandpaper will only touch the highest points unless you make numerous passes over each ridge, steel wool of the proper grade will conform to these multi-ridge surfaces and smooth them with two or three passes total. The only draw-backs to using steel wool are the fine steel hairs that will hang around to annoy you, and the fact that steel wool tends to color things grey, which may not cover as easily with some white paints.

Sanding windows takes time, especially if they are the old double-hung, guillotine type. If your house is equipped with these, here's the foolproof way to get the ones working again that are stuck shut by old coats of paint: Use a three-inch wide putty knife, one that has the blade extending through the handle. Carefully start at one end of the joint between window and frame, and tap the blade of the knife into this joint with a hammer. Do this all the way around the joint. You will probably need to repeat the procedure outside the window. This is the only time I will send you outdoors to do indoor work. This accomplished, gently urge the window open with the heels of your hands against the sash, out towards either side of the frame where it is the strongest. The window may not have been opened for 30 years, but it will respond. You have of course checked that the previous owners have not nailed it shut. If the frame is in good condition, the window will open. If the frame is rotten, and you did not see this earlier, the weakness of the frame will become evident as you try to slide it. Rotten frames are often nailed shut and left alone. Do this or call a carpenter.

If the window is sound but the ropes that counter-balance it have been cut, call a carpenter or replace them yourself. Getting at the ropes and weights is mostly a matter of gently removing the vertical casings right and left of the window itself. The way the casing was fitted together may involve removing a few other pieces first.

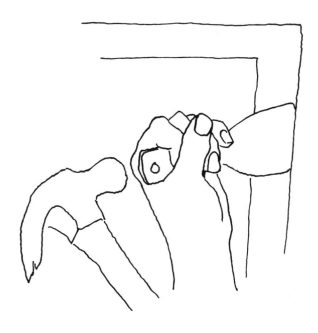

Smoothing wooden window sash, that is the part of the window that touches the glass, requires extra care, because sandpaper scratches glass. Older houses have many scratches. Avoid this by very careful sanding, or better yet, use steel wool. It won't scratch most glass. You should test steel wool on an out-of-the-way piece before starting on your windows. I have never seen medium-coarse steel wool leave marks on glass.

Sometimes walls need a bit of sanding. Textured walls usually do not, because the surface hides imperfections so well. The only time a textured wall will need sanding is when an alteration has been made, and new drywall or plaster has been blended into existing. In this case, the last foot or so from old to new should be sanded lightly, to make the transition more gradual.

It is the smooth wall that shows defects when glossy paint is applied. Smooth walls may require sanding if they have dirt, sand, etc. in the existing coat. Consider buying what is called a sanding pole, a sanding pad attached to a long handle with a rotating joint. The handle can be unscrewed from the pad when using for hand sanding. With the handle in place, this tool has great reach and leverage, allowing you to sand a lot of surface quickly. Sanding the walls of an entire room by hand would take forever. If the smooth, glossy walls in your house have a lot of debris in the existing coat, consider a sanding pole.

My overall approach to sanding is to sand the woodwork and to wash glossy walls with TSP—described in the cleaning section. This would complete the de-glossing of these surfaces if they are smooth enough to your satisfaction as is. However, TSP does not really eliminate the need to sand, especially on trim that receives a lot of wear and tear. For walls and ceilings it is usually satisfactory, although a light pole sanding will increase the strength of the bond between the existing coat and the one you are going to apply.

The procedure for a new smooth wall is to lightly sand between the prime and finish coats. This knocks off whiskers that arise much like those raised when priming wood. A smooth wall shows defects clearly, coated with flat or glossy paint, so a thorough pole sanding between coats with 120 grit is advised. A new textured wall will need little or no sanding, depending on how neatly the texturing worker has done the job. If small spots of new texturing material need to be feathered into existing, a wet sponge also works instead of sandpaper, and leaves no dust. Texturing material, known in the trade as mud, sheds a very fine white powder when sanded. It can be smoothed or removed with a wet sponge. It is easily taken off trim or metal window frames with a wet sponge or rag.

To sum up, sanding large, broad areas is easiest with a pole sander. Walls will need sanding if they are smooth, i.e. not textured, and/or if they are to receive glossy paint. It may be necessary to feather a patch of new texture material into existing with some light sanding. The need to sand existing walls is pretty well limited to sanding out debris and sags in a room where the walls are smooth, and for insuring a strong bond between the enamel coat already in place and the one you are going to apply.

The sandpaper grits that you will use the most when working indoors will be 100 and 120. You should remember that 120 grit is safe on wood trim, while 100 must be followed up with a light sand, using the finer 120.

Filling

On new work, you will need to set any nail heads that are not below the surface as you are filling. A punch to set the nail heads with a hammer is available at the hardware store. The nicest filler for indoor holes is light-weight spackle. It dries fast, cleans up with water, and barely shrinks at all. Simply fill the hole with this material, and wipe across it once or twice with the heel of your hand. Use your finger for pin holes and a putty knife for larger ones. Don't use a wet sponge if you are filling holes in raw wood that you intend to prime that day. A final glance at the spots you have filled tells you if they can be left alone. They should be left smooth with the surface so that they require little or no sanding when they are dry. Rinse your hands frequently.

The ancient Egyptians also developed a very special blue pigment. By 3000 BC this became the highly desirable "Egyptian Blue," and they made so much of it that there was enough left over to export. The heat they needed to produce this color had to be kept within very close tolerances, an achievement that scientists admire today.

Larger holes, deeper or wider, may require a second application but, again, wipe off the filler flush with the surface, don't create extra sanding work for yourself later. Larger holes may actually dry with a bulge, and need a light sanding when dry.

Once the filler has dried, go back over the spots with 120 grit sandpaper and lightly smooth the area, sanding in the same direction as the grain. Raw wood scars very easily, and glossy paint only accentuates the defects.

Filling holes in existing work is about the same. Simply make sure the existing paint around the edges of the hole or dent has been sanded, and what remains still has a firm grip on the wood. Then fill as above.

Light-weight filler is suitable for all holes and also for large defects on vertical surfaces. These defects can include missing areas of one or more layers of paint, deep gouges and scratches, dents in the wood, etc.

When imperfections exist on horizontal surfaces like counter tops or window sills, a stronger filler is needed. Two-part auto body filler has the required strength. It is designed to perform well as a "skin" on auto bodies, with all the bouncing and flexing a car goes through. It can also withstand temperature changes and moisture. It is very suitable for "skimming" surface defects and holding up to the bumps and grinds that horizontal surfaces receive.

If you want to try to get away with using the light-weight filler on high-impact spots, it will work all right for a while, yet a more permanent solution is the auto body filler.

Mixing and using two-part auto body filler is an art in itself. To use this filler you will need some single edge razors (careful!), a three-inch and a one-and-one-half-inch putty knife, and a palette. Best for this is wax paper or a cardboard box with a glossy surface cut into six-inch squares. The idea is to mix the filler on a non-absorbent surface so that the filler will maintain maximum strength. Mixing on newspaper or other porous surface will weaken the filler when part of it gets absorbed into the paper.

With the small putty knife, pull out a dab of the material in the can and wipe it onto the glossy cardboard or wax paper. Then squirt a little of the hardener next to it, following the directions on the can. Keep the two parts separate on the palette, and replace the lid and the cap of both containers.

You should mix only when you are ready to go, because once mixed this material hardens quickly. It handles perfectly for about three minutes, then suddenly it is hard on your knife and useless. So mix small amounts and have the spots you wish to fill lined up in your mind.

If the edge of your putty knife is clean and smooth, you can skim this stuff out to a very thin layer so that it feathers nicely into the area surrounding the defect, and requires minimal sanding later. The wider knife does this easily. Feather carefully while the filler is still wet, because it dries very hard and takes a lot of time to sand down if you have applied too thick a coat.

The large defects we are discussing take two applications of filler to really disappear. Don't fuss over the first layer you apply, just get as much filler into the defect as you can and leave the transition to the surrounding area free of excess.

The really close match to the existing surface comes with the second skim. Auto body filler grips to the first application so well that a very smooth final skim can be obtained. Being careful to leave only an amount that equals the existing surface profile, no more or less, means that the lightest scrape and sand, followed by a spot prime before final coating, will render these types of defects nearly invisible.

When a batch of filler starts to harden, use the single- edge razors to scrape the material off the putty knives so that they are ready to use with the next batch. Dispose of your palette and use a fresh one.

What you are doing with this stuff is pretty amazing. By filling a defect instead of sanding around it in an attempt to conceal it, you are saving time and energy and getting a better finished look. A prime example where skimming works better than sanding is on a door or its frame, right at eye level. Several layers of paint can be chipped away here and there, leaving one- and two-inch wide patches that are below the level of the existing paint. They are "shallow" spots and are very visible, like a scar. By carefully skimming such a spot with two coats of filler followed by a gentle sanding, it blends in with the surrounding surface and no longer shows. Sanding down the edges of such a defect would never conceal it as completely as skimming it.

Outdoors, where weather is a major factor, oil primer is forced into holes and allowed to dry before the holes are filled. This assures that the filling material won't dry, shrink, and fail quickly, because the primed wood inside the hole won't suck the moisture out of the filling material, turning it to dust. It is also done so that even the inside of the hole is primed against moisture when the filling material eventually starts to crack due to sun, rain, and cold.

Indoors, moist conditions exist in all bathrooms, laundry rooms, and kitchens. You may also wish to prime in all holes before you fill them. Spackle will last indoors if you don't prime inside the holes first, but it will last longer if you do, especially in these moist parts of the house.

If you encounter a wide hole in drywall, where there is nothing behind the hole to pack your filler against, there is an easy trick to use. Steel wool can often be stuffed into such a hole, just far enough below the surface to act as a backing when you skim filler over it.

If you have an extra wide hole in drywall, get a stick of wood that is longer than the hole is wide, and pass it through the hole in the wall. Use a soft piece of wood that will take screws easily, like pine or fir. You will also need some two-inch drywall screws. You can hold the stick in place inside the wall using your finger, or by driving a screw into the middle of the stick first, to use as a little handle that you can grip onto with a pair of pliers. Then drive screws through the wall and into both ends of the stick, leaving them snug so they are below the wall surface and can be filled later. Spin out the screw you used as a little handle, and you have a backing to pack the filler against. If the hole is still too wide to fill, you can cut a piece of plywood so that it will fit in the hole. Secure it in place by running a screw through it into the stick. This piece of plywood should be thin enough to be slightly below the surface of the wall, so that you can easily skim filler over the defect and feather it in with the surrounding area later.

Priming

My definition of priming is sealing against moisture, closing the pores of a surface so that it has a waterproof base for the next coat of paint to grip onto. Paints referred to as primers all have this ability to seal a surface.

Early societies painted a lot of their stone sculpture and buildings with bright colors. A few known examples include the Egyptians, Greeks, Romans, and Mayans, among many others.

Every large paint company will have different primers formulated for every conceivable surface situation. Their specialization here is warranted, because the prime coat makes or breaks the life of a paint job. There are different primers for interior or exterior wood, plaster, different metals, plastics, etc. The technology has evolved to the point that you can count on a long-lasting bond if you use the right primer for a given surface.

For interior work I recommend an oil base primer for wood. It penetrates the pores and locks into the wood, and sands very nicely. For new drywall or plaster, the common primer is generically known as PVA, a water-based poly-vinyl material that dries to a plastic film and effectively seals the pores of the wallboard and texturing material.

You must also spray white shellac on all knots in the wood you are going to paint. This holds back the pitch in the knot so that it doesn't bleed through the paint and yellow over time. Spray all knots on bare wood, and any that show through on existing wood. While you're at it, spray any ink and letters from the lumber yard that you can see on new wood.

In priming new work the key is to get everything coated. Don't miss a spot, because it will show through later as a dull spot in your enamel. You are sealing the wood or plaster, so that your enamel coat has an evenly sealed foundation to grip onto.

Apply primer with the same care that you would apply finish paint, so you don't leave sloppy brush or roller marks. These will show through after your final coat if you are sloppy. You will probably be sanding after the prime coat to remove the roughness of the wood or plaster, but take a minute to blend the brush or roller strokes evenly as you prime, so that you don't have to spend extra time sanding them out.

On existing work a firmly bonded enamel coat that is already in place, once it has been thoroughly sanded to dull the gloss, will act as a primer coat. In this case, only a "spot-prime" is necessary on any porous spots, such as bare wood or places that you have filled, to assure a uniformly glossy enamel finish. Shellac in a spray-can works as a spot-primer prior to finish coating, and it dries in about 20 minutes. Read the can for exact drying time.

When priming places that are to receive enamel, remember that any porous spots you miss will show through as dull spots in the finish coat. This is the nature of all gloss paints, oil or latex, and thorough priming assures a uniform looking finish coat.

Another priming situation involves applying two coats of paint, but the first coat is not necessarily to seal the surface and it is not necessarily "primer" paint. I am describing a previously painted room where you are going to make an extreme color change, lighter or darker, and one finish coat will not completely "hide" the existing color. For example, if it is wall of flat latex, two coats of flat wall paint will probably achieve the desired "hide."

If you plan a big color change on enamel trim or glossy walls, and it will take two coats to do it, it is better to use an actual primer paint for the first coat, after dulling the gloss of the existing enamel with 120 grit sandpaper. The reason for this is that the primer grabs onto a newly sanded surface extremely well, and your second (finish) coat will then grip the primer much better than it would itself, had you used the enamel for both coats. Plus, little or no sanding is needed between the primer and top coat, which would not have been the case had you used the enamel first.

To assure complete hide when making a major color change, use two coats of flat wall paint on flat walls, but use an actual primer as your first coat on any surface that is to receive an enamel top-coat.

Another trick for assuring complete hide is to be aware of how well a chosen color will cover. Expecting to finish coat something and finding out that it will take two coats is frustrating. As mentioned above, if it is an enamel section that requires two coats, better to make the first coat actual primer and avoid an extra sanding step. The trick when you are double-coating is to have your primer tinted at the paint store so that it is close to your finish color. This way your top coat is guaranteed to cover beautifully. Undercoating with a tinted primer makes the finish color rich and full, because it isn't barely hiding a contrasting color underneath, it is working with the color underneath it to look rich and full-bodied. Tinting your primer makes the job easier because the paint covers better and yields nicer finish results.

Talk with the paint salesperson so that you don't tint the primer to the exact color of your finish coat. This way you can see the difference between coats as you are finish coating, and it is easier to see where you have skipped a spot as you are working.

Caulking

Caulking is very satisfying because you can see immediately the dramatic improvement you are making.

The idea is to caulk every crack in the trim, and every crack between the trim and wall, before you finish coat. A lot of trim gets painted white or off-white, and black cracks really show. Caulking them first is easy and gives your trim a sharp, rich finished look.

I recommend latex caulk with silicone. It handles easily, thins with water, and takes paint extremely well. Read the label, however, to make sure that it is paintable.

Snip off the tip of the caulk tube at an angle. Then break the seal that lies between the base of the tip and the top of the tube. Use a 16d finish nail to pass through the hole in the tip and perforate this seal in a few places.

Caulk guns have a trigger and a pressure release. It doesn't take long to get the feel for applying caulk. The main trick is to time how much caulk is coming out with how quickly you pass the tip over the

Scarcity of linseed oil in Germany during and after World War Two led to the development of modern latex there. Scarcity of natural rubber in the U.S. led to the development of latex around the same time.

length of the crack. The width of this bead can be altered depending upon how much of the plastic tip you have cut away. If you forget to release the pressure on the plunger of the gun, caulk will continue to extrude from the tip. Not releasing the pressure at the end of a pass is a habit you will quickly break as gobs of caulk begin to accumulate at your feet.

Step one is getting the caulk applied into the crack. Next, run your finger the length of the crack to press it in and smooth the transition from caulk to wood. After a bit of this you will get a feel for how much is necessary to close the gap, yet leave little or no excess. If too much has been applied, gently wipe the length of the crack with your wet rag, then smooth with your finger again. Check the area to be sure the joint is smooth and has no ridges from your finger. It can then be left to dry; two hours is usually enough on a sunny day. Too little caulk will shrink to the point where a second application will be required. Too much caulk takes extra time in wiping away the excess. I can only tell you the moves; the knack comes from actually doing it.

A little practice shows you how quick and easy caulking is. Since it cleans up with water, don't be hesitant to get right at it. You can always wipe an area clean and start over if it becomes a mess.

Where two cracks that you are filling meet at a corner, the edge of a putty knife, combined with dabbing with your finger and a wet rag, can get it looking right. Just try to close the crack and leave the caulk even enough so it will look neat when it is finish coated. Remember that the caulk shrinks a bit as it dries,so leave a slightly curved bead in the joints you are filling. This way the bead dries without opening again, and a uniform look remains.

Large cracks will require two applications. Get as much caulk into the opening as you can, then wipe flush with the wet rag. When dry, a second coat will usually caulk it up flush. Extremely wide openings may require forcing pieces of wood into them before caulking, to take up most of the space. Less caulk will be needed. If you can fit a piece of wooden stir-stick into the void, and get it to stay just below the surface, then one application of caulk should dry flush. It will now be ready for finish coating.

Dry caulk does not sand well. Remove extra caulk with a wet rag as you go. Any gobs that you miss can be gently scraped or cut away when dry. Better yet, that final careful glance over the area that you have just caulked will save you the need to remove any dried, stubborn caulk later.

Cleaning

You want to make sure that all surfaces are free of anything that will keep paint from sticking properly. Crayon has got to go—paint thinner on a rag removes this. Wax from candles has got to go—a putty knife and several pieces of sandpaper remove this. Ink and water stains are sprayed with a stain sealer. Shellac, white or clear, is the common thing used to seal stains. It is available in spray cans at your paint store.

All gloss walls must be washed before they are re-painted. For this use TSP, a powerful cleaner available at paint stores. Following the directions on the container, mix up a batch in a large bucket, using hot water. Use a standard kitchen sponge mop so that the long handle does the reaching for you.

Before you start, clear all counters of food and objects. There is no need to protect tile or wood floors from TSP, as long as you do a quick mop rinse over the floors and counters as soon as you have finished cleaning the ceilings and walls. Cover your head and use gloves and eye protection. TSP is strong and requires these precautions. Once you use it you will see that it is worth the trouble. Washing with TSP assures that you are not trapping an oily film between coats of paint. This will add years to the endurance of your paint job.

Most rooms with gloss walls, that is bathrooms, kitchens, and laundry rooms, have a sink or tub in them. This is handy for rinsing away dirt from your sponge. You could use a rinse bucket, but you would be re-filling it with fresh water very often. I just rinse the mop in the sink or tub before I rinse the wall or ceiling surface, and before I plunge the mop back into the TSP bucket. This keeps the TSP mixture pretty clean, so that I'm not re-applying dirt to the walls and ceilings.

Use of the sponge mop often eliminates the need to use a ladder, because of the long reach the handle provides. Corners or tight spots may benefit from using a hand-held sponge, especially when rinsing.

Start with the ceiling. Wet a large area with TSP. Always keep a section ahead of you wet with the chemical, giving it time to lift the dirt for you. Three minutes is plenty. Then rinse the mop and use the clean mop to swab that section of the ceiling. The rhythm of this job goes: wet an area, let the chemical break down the dirt, wipe off the dirt with a clean sponge, then rinse the surface again. Bathroom and kitchen walls really collect grime over the years. You can tell when you have rinsed away most of the film when the mop no longer leaves streaks as you rinse. Use the same steps on the walls, working from the top down. When you are finished, remember to wipe down all adjacent surfaces that you didn't TSP, to remove splashes of the cleaning mixture and dirty drips.

Another cleaning topic is mold. Mold develops in bathrooms with poor ventilation, parts of the house that receive little sunlight, anywhere during rainy season, etc. It can be removed with bleach and hot water. This will kill the surface mold, but it won't remove the cause. The best a painter can do is to kill existing mold with bleach and add a mold preventive to the paint being applied. This comes in pre-measured packs and can be mixed into each gallon at your paint store. If you have a serious mold problem, ask at the paint store for any special suggestions or products that they might have.

Cleaning also includes brushing off all dust from surfaces before you apply the paint. Special attention should be paid to removing dust from any surface that you are going to enamel, because bits of dirt show up quite readily in a coat of glossy paint. A separate dust brush is used for this purpose, and it need not be expensive. Three inches wide is about right. Also, a great help is a vacuum cleaner with a little brush attachment at the end of the hose. This lifts debris out of the corners that the brush can't quite get. Start at the top of the section to be painted and work down, using the dust brush and the vacuum cleaner together. I also run my hand over a surface one last time just before I enamel it, to remove the last bits of dust that remain. For a perfect, dust-free surface, especially wood, you can use disposable tack cloths that act as dust magnets. Paint stores carry them. They work great on surfaces but can't beat the vacuum cleaner at removing dust from corners and tight spots.

For walls, you can slap at them with a large rag, and use a broom to knock down dust and spider webs that have collected. As always, wear a mask during all dusty operations.

A last detail at this point is to remove all the switch plates and plug covers. Screw each screw back into its hole in the wall a couple of turns when the plate is removed. That way the screws can't get lost. Throw all the plates from that room in the sink and wash them with soap and warm water. Then keep the set from each room together until the painting is done and they can be put back in place.

Handling Paint

When you control the paint and keep it from getting messy, the whole job becomes a lot easier. Get a good start by setting up a small area in the corner of a porch, garage, or a room with no rug. Lay down a drop cloth or plenty of newspaper and do all your mixing and pouring here.

The oldest known use of paint can be seen on the walls of caves in Altamira, Spain and Lascaux, France. These "paintings" are tens of thousands of years old.

Working out of a clean plastic bucket (minimum one gallon) keeps brushing under control. Pour an inch of the paint you are using into this bucket, wipe the side and the rim of the paint can with your brush, and replace the lid. Gently push down the lid with the heels of your hands. Leave the lid snug, yet easy to pry off later when you need more paint. Don't hammer shut the lid of a paint can until the end of a job, and then only when you have wiped the rim clean of paint. If there is paint in the rim when you hammer the lid down, the paint will splatter in all directions. If you puncture the rim in four or five places with a nail before you start, the rim will drain by itself.

Now for a priceless trick of the trade: keep your paint flowing nicely with products made for this purpose. I'm not referring here to paint thinner, or water when using latex, but to paint "additives," formulated for oil or latex. They replenish the part of your paint that is starting to evaporate. If you add paint thinner to oil paint when it gets sticky, it will flow from the brush better, but it will also be runnier, more prone to sag, and not cover as well. However, if you add pure linseed oil to restore the flow, your paint will flow nicely again without losing its body. It will handle like "fresh" paint instead of "thin" paint. When added to a primer, extra oil will help the paint to penetrate the wood and lock into the pores better, increasing the life of the paint job. Ask at your paint store for details.

This is a tip you should try, because once you realize you can keep your paint "just right" the entire time you are brushing, the job becomes a lot nicer. I think many people decide that they don't like painting due to the frustration of trying to brush paint that has become too thick to use easily.

Remember that in some states, environmental laws apply to certain practices when mixing paints, especially the oil-based ones. Ask your paint dealer about the applicable laws where you live.

Consider buying a pro-quality brush to paint trim and doors. The job will turn out smoother than with a cheap brush. I will tell you how to clean brushes so that you can use them again and again. Cheap brushes tend to streak and leave brush marks in the paint. After all your careful preparation, you owe it to yourself to have the painted surface look as nice as possible when you're done. After all, it will last for years, so why not be happy with it?

A three-inch brush is common for professional painters, yet if you are not practiced with handling a brush, you may wish to start with a couple of angled two-inch brushes, one for oil and one for latex. When you have gotten used to these, you may wish to try your hand at the larger size brush.

When you do the same thing for countless hours you develop your own techniques. The knack acquired through actual brushing cannot be taught. The best I can do is share the moves with you that work best for me. In brushing you are doing two things—you are getting the paint onto the surface from the bucket, and then you are brushing it out to a level surface and leaving the brush marks uniform and attractive. This second step is called laying off the paint. What I do is to dip my brush into the bucket, and tap it against the inside. This leaves about as much paint in the brush as you can handle without drips. Do not wipe the brush off on the rim of the bucket, tap it against the inside. This way, the rim of your bucket won't be lined with wet paint that starts to spread against the handle and your hands. Keep things from getting sticky.

Using a full brush allows you to get a lot of paint out of the bucket and onto the surface quickly. Always apply paint with the full width of the brush. A brush can distribute paint to many different levels of wood in the same stroke. This seems so simple yet it is surprising how many people have picked up the time-wasting habit of turning the brush on edge to paint the different "steps" of a piece of trim, one at a time. Plenty of paint applied using the full face of the brush coats trim very rapidly.

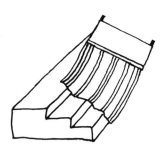

Laying off trim work is a different story. Laying off refers to the final gentle stroke of the paint brush before you leave a given section to dry. I will describe this technique in detail in a moment. Once the surface is wet for a given section, you must lay off each tier of the trim profile separately. The brush's same "reach around" ability that works for you when you are applying paint works against you when you are laying it off with the final touch. This results in brush marks that are not smooth and consistent, and can also leave thins that allow the previous coat to show through. The way to avoid this is to pass the bristles along each tier separately, being careful to use the brush in such a way that the bristles behave.

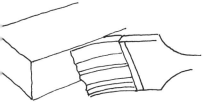

Keep the bristles from reaching around the edge and messing up a surface you have already laid off.

Rather than working over a small area at a time, perfecting it and then repeating, I first get enough paint onto a good sized section, three or four feet of trim for example, then lay off the larger section. This is a faster way to work, and you are overlapping in fewer places because each section is much larger.

It goes like this—first get an entire section wet with paint, not necessarily perfectly coated, but wet. This goes very quickly. Then come back over the area with a slightly "drier" brush and stroke out the surface. A dry brush is achieved by wiping most of the paint against the rim of your bucket. If you wipe the brush against the same general spot on the rim when you need a drier brush, the paint is less likely to spread onto the brush handle and your hands.

As you stroke out a section, the paint gets evenly distributed, and if the paint color contains enough "hide", the coat starts to look uniform. You can tell that the whole surface is coated when the color looks even throughout the entire section. At this point I lay off each section one final time, to leave all the brush strokes in an even line. With properly flowing paint this process works perfectly.

Laying off is the moment when all your prep and finish coating come together, and when you step away from this final touch, your trim is completed. For this reason, I look pretty carefully at each section before I move on. Thin spots, drips, poor brush strokes, all these things can be resolved at this point very easily. Once the coat starts to dry, however, touching up doesn't blend in very well. So this final light laying off move is one I always do slowly and carefully.

Never start a laying off stroke by placing your bristles in the middle of a section. This leaves a real valley, and often this spot is so thin that it dries with the previous color showing through. Instead, feather the finish coat back into itself as you go, ending your stroke by lifting away where the sections overlap, not by dropping the brush into a section you have already laid off. Placing your brush at the end of a section, or in a corner, and stroking from there, leaves the nicest looking strokes when the paint dries.

Laying off is a very gentle thing. Picture a gravel path that you have just raked every which way. Now for the last touch, you gently pull the rake over just the top layer of gravel, carefully in even, straight lines, blending each stroke into the previous one so that the path is a series of continuous lines. You don't need to force the rake down deep into the gravel to get this effect. A gentle pull over just the top layer achieves the look.

Now paint is not as coarse as gravel, but the comparison is appropriate. Paint is a liquid, yet grainier than you may think, especially when compared to varnish, for instance. Varnish can run and sag like water, where paint does these things slowly and less often.

A sag or run occurs where you have applied too much paint to a certain area and gravity takes over. Sags can be removed very easily with a dry brush. As you are painting, simply glance back over your work every 15 minutes or so. The most likely places for sags to appear are where verticals meet horizontals. If you have applied too much paint to any vertical, it will accumulate and run out at the bottom corner.

These vertical/horizontal intersections are tricky in another way. Any time you pass a brush at right angles across any protruding ridge, paint will be left there to sag. What you need to do is to stroke in the opposite direction, or just be careful as you pass these junctions.

Sags are common where a brushing blunder has been made around the edges of objects. Stroking your brush firmly against the rim of your bucket removes excess paint. Doing this against the edge of something you are painting, even gently, sends paint drooling down the side. So carry your brush across a surface and off the edge gently, rather than creating a major sag by stroking in the other direction.

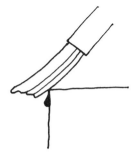

This is the main cause of sags when brushing. It is best to break this habit.

When handling a brush it is useful to remember that most of the paint is always up in your brush and not out at the tip of your bristles. When the tips of your bristles are dry, the brush is still loaded with paint further up. That's why using the full face of the brush coats so quickly. The tips of the bristles are used more when laying off the final stroke. As you work, you always have this reserve of paint stored in the upper part of your brush. So you can put this upper region to work in certain situations. I use it on the sides of doors and skinny trim pieces, especially window sash.

By lightly "slapping" the edge of things with the upper part of the brush, paint is applied quickly without excess being sent around the corners where it is unwanted. This is a quick way to apply paint to these spots, followed by a gentle laying off stroke.

You want to be sure to wipe the extra paint out of this upper part of the brush now and then, against the rim of your bucket. Too much paint build-up leads to flying drips and paint running down the handle and onto your hands, which is no fun. This happens even faster when you are brushing overhead.

When applying paint, human and animal hairs always appear in the finish coat, as do bristles from your brush. Simply remove the excess paint from your brush and then stab out the hair with the tip of your brush, at right angles to the direction the hair is lying. It will pop right out of there and you can easily pick it off the tip of the bristles with your fingers. Then simply stroke over the area from which the hair has been removed, and feather the finish coat into the surrounding area.

Cutting In

My definition of "cutting in" is drawing an even, attractive line between two areas that differ in color and/or type of paint, such as where flat wall paint meets semi-gloss trim paint, or where a white ceiling meets a tan wall. It also refers to using a brush to get paint well into corners before coming through with a roller.

The thing to do is to cut in a tricky edge only once. This is done by executing the painting steps in their proper order. This sequence worked well for me over the years: cut in and roll the ceilings and walls, brush all the trim, then cut in the borders around the trim. All the places where trim meets wall have already been caulked. As you enamel the trim, make sure that you carry the paint at least to the caulk, or a bit past it and onto the wall. No need to leave a perfect edge, just make sure that the trim paint at least covers the caulked joint.

When that dries, come back through with the wall paint and cut in around the trim. It is faster and easier to control your brush when you are cutting in a broad surface. One reason for this is that when turned on edge, a brush is flexed more than when you pass it over a surface using the broad side. Also, the less angle between the brush handle and the surface you are brushing, the less flex the bristles undergo. When the bristles are bent, they tend to push harder against the surface you are trying to coat, like a mild spring. As a result, paint will not properly cover what's underneath unless the laying-off stroke is gentle, with the bristles barely flexed at all.

Approach cutting in boldly. The way to get paint up to an edge quickly is with the side of the brush, then to lay off with the full face of the brush. You will take forever and get frustrated if you try to place a brush full of paint right against an edge you are trying to cut in. The way to do it is to take the full brush and pass it several inches from the junction, parallel to it. Distribute a supply of paint evenly along this line, several inches away from the junction, not directly into it. Two dips in the bucket should give you two or three feet of paint in this region. Now, with a drier brush make your pass right up to the joint. The idea at this stage is to get the wall wet with paint, not fully hidden. Move along the joint the distance that you have already distributed paint, drawing small amounts of this reserve down to the edge until the wall is wet. Then, using the broad full face of the brush, pass along the joint to lay it off until the section is uniformly coated, that is, looks like one continuous color.

When cutting in, if most of your paint is on the wall and not out at the tips of your bristles, you can lay the brush sideways up to the joint you are cutting in, so that the tip of the bristles lightly touch the trim, or whatever you are trying to keep free of paint. That is, you can actually use the thing you are cutting up to as a guide for a straight line, if the tips of your bristles are pretty dry. That's why I cut right to the junction with my brush on edge with just enough paint to wet the wall. When I pass over again, pulling the reserve paint up to the seam to assure complete hide, and then stroking with the brush laid full face, the paint will grab more readily. The trim will be free of unwanted paint.

Now read this section again and study the illustrations carefully, because I have just described the easiest way to do the hardest part of housepainting.

Cutting in against trim that is the same color is much easier than cutting a gray wall up to white trim, for example. Slight errors show much more when the two surfaces you are drawing a line between contrast in color. Cutting in such contrasting surfaces takes longer than cutting in similar colors.

A.

B.

C.

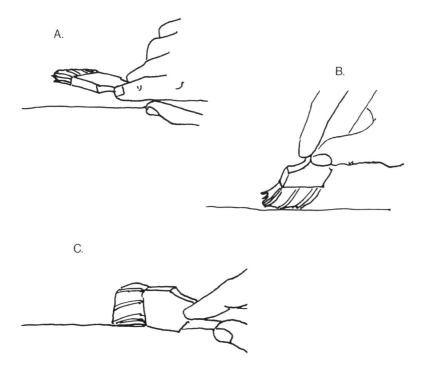

A one-and-a-half inch latex brush is perfect for cutting in. It is easy to keep the bristles under control as you move past the edge with this size brush.

Cutting in seems a bit intimidating at first, but when you follow the steps that I have listed, a lot of the worry goes out of it. Taping off with masking tape takes time and doesn't always work. Even if it is put carefully in place at the exact spots where you want the paint to stop, there is still no guarantee that the paint won't seep behind it and cause further work and time. So my approach is to cut in the way I have described, and have a wet rag close by for the occasional blunders that come from being human.

I only use masking tape to protect baseboards and other trim when I am rolling, by slapping it over trim to keep the roller mist off. You may say that a professional painter has so much practice that of course it seems easier to cut in by hand, and not use masking tape. I suggest that you try both ways on a section where you can comfortably experiment, and simply have a wet rag in a clean bucket at hand, or a rag and some thinner, if you are using oil-based paints. Experiment and get the feel for what works the best for you. Be bold as you cut in. It goes faster that way, and you can always wipe a spot with the rag should you mess up. I always paint with a rag close at hand, to correct mistakes right away and move on.

Cutting in corners that are to receive the same paint is a lot easier. All you are doing here is to apply paint several inches out from the corner in both directions with your brush, so that when you come through with the roller you will roll to this pre-cut boundary and stop.

Rolling

Rolling flat latex is the fastest and least likely to show defects of any interior painting operation. With proper drop cloths and masking tape to catch the inevitable fine mist that a roller spins off, rolling a room yields quick results. Old bed sheets or thin plastic drop cloths are best used to keep drips and spray off furniture. Canvas drop cloths are best for the floor, because paint dries more quickly on canvas, and you won't get paint on the bottom of your shoes as easily. A canvas drop at least eight feet square, and a "runner" three by eight feet, will provide you with the necessary floor protection. Disposable drop cloths of similar dimensions will do the job.

Furniture should be gathered in the center of the room if possible, and completely covered with drop cloths. If very heavy pieces of furniture are in the room, get them three feet from the wall and covered so that you can paint the wall behind them with relative ease. Protect the trim with two-inch wide masking tape: baseboards, tops of windows and doors. Tape some newspaper to window sills, and lay plastic, newspaper, or a drop cloth on counter tops and bookcases. In all doorways, lay some protection on the floor several feet into the next room, because roller mist gets carried by the slightest draft in the house, and seldom falls straight down. Once your preparation is complete and your trim, carpets and furniture safe, you are ready to begin.

You will cut in around the trim at the very end, so the only corners you need cut in at first are the corners of the room and where the walls meet the ceiling. Paint a good thick coat with your brush at least two inches out from the corner in both directions, then make a firm last stroke across the edge of the section you have just cut in, to feather the wet paint into the dry wall beyond it. This way a ridge won't dry there. In a room where the ceiling is the same color as the walls, you end up with two-inch borders cut in where the walls meet the ceiling and in all four corners of the room. If there are any alcoves or bays, the corners of these should be cut in also.

If you are not going to paint the ceiling, you will carefully cut up to it as you cut in the corners of the room. Rolling just the walls requires using drop cloths at least three feet out from the walls. In this case, the furniture and floor in the middle of the room are less threatened by paint drips, since you won't be rolling the ceiling over them.

If you are using a different color on the ceiling, your first step is to brush paint around the ceiling edges. Make sure it is at least to the wall, better yet a bit on it. This way you will move quickly, getting the border of the ceiling completely covered. Only later, when the ceiling is dry and you prepare to roll the walls, will you spend time carefully brushing this junction with the wall color, to maintain a straight and attractive edge. Remember, only cut in a tricky edge once.

The ceiling can be rolled at the same time as the walls if you are using the same color throughout. If you are using a lighter color for the ceiling, it must be rolled first and allowed to dry before you begin the walls. Let me describe rolling the walls, and the complete picture will become clear.

I must tell you that the common roller tray is not used by painters. Instead, we use a five-gallon plastic bucket, available from the paint store for next to nothing. Trays hold very little paint, so they need refilling constantly, and are easy to step in if placed on the floor. The five-gallon bucket, with a gallon or so of paint in the bottom, along with a screen set in place inside the bucket to control the amount of paint your roller contains, will make your job much faster and far less messy. Use a tray with a liner if you must, but if you have any amount of rolling to do, I can't recommend strongly enough that you try the bucket technique.

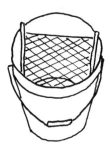

Your trim is protected with masking tape to keep off the roller mist. Your bucket and roller, with roller extension handle, are ready to go, and you have a runner drop cloth in place. Put your bucket on this drop and work from the floor beyond it. Drop cloths shield the floor or carpet from paint, but if you walk on and off the drop cloth as you are working you will track drips from the cloth onto the carpet or floor. The best way to avoid this is to pay attention. Stay off the drop cloth as much as possible. With the extension handle you are working far enough away from the wall to avoid this problem.

If you feel more comfortable using a roller without an extension handle, the following section will still give you a few ideas on efficient rolling. In hallways and tight spots, a handle is useless, anyway.

I like to get three or four full roller's worth of paint onto the wall from near the ceiling down to near the baseboard, a vertical line of paint for each dip into the bucket. Roughly a roller's width can separate these three or four vertical paths of paint. Since the roller is nine inches wide, you have set yourself up to roll the wall from floor to ceiling and about six feet wide. Next, use the roller to distribute the paint until the entire section is wet. Long strokes from floor to ceiling do this very quickly. If the roller gets a little dry, reach ahead to a wetter patch and pull the paint over to where it is needed.

Use care as you roll up to the ceiling, especially if it is a different color. Slow your stroke there and at the baseboard. Stop about three inches shy of the baseboard, since you will come through later with a brush to cut up to the baseboard and fill in this unpainted strip, after you have painted the baseboard. The next trick is to tilt your roller and roll it on the wall a couple of feet to remove the excess from the roller's ends. This way you won't trail a raised ridge as you pass over the surface one last time.

Re-roll the entire section slow and steady, moving over half a roller width at the end of each vertical stroke. This does the final thorough, even coating that will result in a wall that has no skips or thin patches in the paint when it dries. Any less methodical system of rolling will probably leave skips. Working across a section like a farmer tilling a field will assure that you have passed the roller over every square inch of the wall three times using the above technique. It also lets you know where you've been, and leaves the surface free of the ridges that result from careless rolling.

Tom Sawyer convinced people on the street that it was a privilege worth paying for to whitewash a fence.

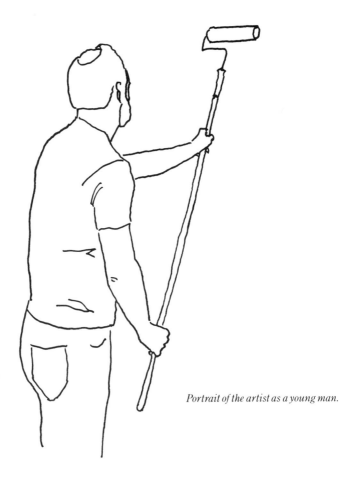

Portrait of the artist as a young man.

I find that rolling a section, floor to ceiling and about six feet wide, takes about three minutes. And with the extension handle, you exert far less energy and needn't stoop over. Summary: get three or four roller's worth onto the wall, stroke it out until the entire section is wet, roll one last time half width at a time.

The next section of wall is a repeat of this process. The last couple feet of your previous section may be a bit thin, so overlap your previous section two roller widths, to insure enough paint there. As you roll a ceiling, overlap the sections in this way as you work, for the same reason.

I roll a two- or three-foot perimeter of the ceiling as I am rolling the walls, provided the same color is being used. I do the entire room this way, then use my broad drop cloth and complete the ceiling. Quality flat wall paints dry so evenly that you can get away with this approach. Gloss paints are a different story. With gloss paints, you are better off to roll the ceiling and each wall separately, always overlapping at a wet edge, as the paint cans often advise. Otherwise the junction where the paint meets a drier section will show up differently. It will be duller or shinier than the rest of the wall or ceiling. This is called flashing, and the way to avoid it is to work one surface at a time and to always overlap one section into another as soon as you can. Again, this only applies to gloss paints, and the cheap flat ones. Quality flat wall paint dries so evenly that it is almost impossible to have an unsatisfactory appearance when it dries.

One last subject when rolling, and a big one, is acoustic ceilings. I am here to tell you that rolling acoustic ceilings works. It is a neat trick to brighten up any room that suffers from the presence of these strange relics from the past. Often referred to as "cottage cheese" ceilings, they are everywhere. They are usually left alone because people think that they can't be rolled, and that spraying is too much trouble. So they are dark from neglect and often make a room feel like a cave.

The solution is easy, if you completely cover the floor of the room and work carefully. Best to remove the furniture if you can. All you need is the normal five-gallon bucket set-up, but using a roller cover designed specifically for acoustic ceilings. Use quality flat wall paint, and thin your paint a lot with water, one part water to three parts paint. The paint will soak into the irregular surface of the acoustic material very readily when it has been thinned to this degree, but you must move carefully as you work. Pressing the roller too hard against the ceiling, when it is full of thinned paint, will result in a downpour. Instead, roll gently over the ceiling with a full roller, allowing the ceiling to draw the paint out of the roller, and you will avoid this problem.

The reason I thin the paint so much to roll an acoustic ceiling is that you can run into problems using full-strength paint. The water helps the paint soak in. The thinned paint is not sticky, and it won't start pulling away the acoustic material. The paint bucket will start to get full of individual puffs from the ceiling, but the surface won't start to pull away. Two coats are necessary, but you will be glad you took the trouble when you see how much brighter and open the room feels when you are finished. Wait four hours before your second coat.

Use the roller to coat the ceiling all the way into the corner where it meets the wall. You will get ceiling paint on the top three inches of the wall this way, so use your brush to remove the excess as you proceed. Trying to dab paint up into this corner will drive you crazy, so use the roller. The only place I dab with the brush is where the ceiling meets the four corners of the room, and around the ceiling light fixture. Don't try painting the acoustic ceiling in a room unless you plan to re-paint the walls.

Use an off-white with a lot of hiding power, as discussed in the section on choosing paint colors. Also, plan to store the ceiling paint in its own can, because it will contain a good amount of cottage cheese when you are finished. Happy rolling!

Windows

The main problem when painting windows is keeping the paint off the glass. There are a number of ways to do this, and they all take time. One way is to cut in against the glass by hand, leaving a six-teenth-inch border of paint on the glass to act as a seal at the glass/wood junction. Pros do this, and their experience keeps them quick at it.

You could use masking tape, but I feel the results aren't worth the time you spend, because tape never really leaves a clean line, and actually lets paint creep behind it in spots. You could brush the window in the time it takes to tape it off.

My technique is crude but effective. I brush the window rapidly, getting a full coat everywhere, and spending little time trying to keep the paint off the glass. This takes far less time than any other approach. Add to it the time I spend later cleaning the glass with single-edge razors, and the time per window is still very close, yet I haven't spent the concentrated, steady energy that is necessary to cut in each window pane carefully. When you are brushing a couple rooms' worth of windows, this fatigue factor can really slow you down if you don't enjoy the tedious effort of keeping paint from the glass.

One plus with this technique is that it enables you to get a full coat right up to the glass, and even into the small cracks and gaps found where the wood meets the panes. This adds to the final sharp appearance after you come through later with the razor blade, and achieves the seal by forcing the paint down into this junction.

One minus with this technique is that it requires handling razor blades, which require caution when you use and dispose of them, especially if small children are around the house. Also, I hear it is possible to scratch glass with a razor blade, and some window manufacturers advise against using blades on their windows at all. Just like when you prep near glass, test an out-of-the-way spot before you start scraping with a razor. I have never seen blades scratch glass in the hundreds of windows I have painted. I think it is because I am careful, and I start with a fresh, sharp single-edge razor every window or so. Stores sell razor blade holders that make the job of scraping easier and safer.

Let me repeat: Razors can be dangerous if you are not careful when using them and disposing of them. Be responsible with razors, or don't use them.

You may wish to use a combination of techniques to keep the glass clean: Brush the wood more carefully, and catch the inevitable error with a rag before it dries, or leave the occasional blunder for the razor.

There are several ways to end up with clean glass, as you can see. I think you should use the approach that you feel most comfortable with. If your home does not have a lot of multi-pane windows, it won't take that long to carefully cut in against the glass. When you have complex windows, the above considerations should be taken into account, since the total time they will take to paint may be substantial.

Double-hung windows are common, and in the sanding section I discussed how to get them to open if they are stuck shut. You have to be able to get both upper and lower sections of these windows to move if you want to re-paint them entirely. If both windows will not move far enough to allow the necessary access to the upper one, try to free them if you can. If not, or if one or both of them are nailed shut, then all you can do is to paint them as is. Try to keep too much paint from building up at the edge of the window where it slides in the vertical channels. This is the spot you forced the putty knife into to free the window in the first place. Once you have coated the upper window entirely, leave the bottom window open slightly so that you can paint it all the way to its lower edge. Since a window stays open in warm weather, if you painted it in the closed position it will look unfinished when open. A light push with the hands when the window has dried will break the light paint seal that usually remains in the track where the window slides.

To be able to entirely paint double-hung windows, you need to slide the sections of the window past each other, to the point where the upper window's bottom section is accessible. This is the only way to reach that part of a double-hung window, and often this spot has been neglected over the years and looks pretty sloppy. Any time you open a double-hung window, this bottom piece of the upper window shows. That's why it pays to gain access to this spot when painting, so that a complete finish coat remains.

On the left the double-hung windows are closed. On the right they are slid past each other to paint. Note that the upper window is in black to show the idea clearly.

You want to paint all of the upper window that you can reach with the windows slid past each other. Then slide them back almost to their normal places, an inch or two short of closed. At this point you have access to the rest of both windows, and after you brush them you can leave them as they are to dry. If it is a breezy day, don't coat the window sill until the windows have dried enough to close, so that the wind doesn't deposit dirt in the paint on the sill.

The vertical tracks left and right that double-hung windows slide in are usually not painted, so that the windows continue to slide easily. You will notice on older houses that sloppy painters have left paint blunders here. You can gently scrape the errors off, or live with them. If you paint this track, it will get scraped up every time you raise and lower the window. They look better if left unpainted.

A few details for multi-pane windows: First, I brush the wood between the panes. These pieces of wood are called mullions. As I complete the wood around two adjacent panes, I lightly slap the top edge of the piece dividing them with my brush. This leaves enough paint on there to gently lay off. When the mullions are done, I brush the perimeter of the window. This way I have a continuous, non-sticky time of it on the most visible part of the window, the broader perimeter.

A.   B.

C.   D.

Brushing a window with only one pane is simply a matter of top, sides, and bottom. The other common window style, the casement window, is also very easy to paint. This is the window that opens like a door when you spin the hand crank. Here you simply paint the perimeter and the edge that faces you when the window is swung fully open.

When you have brand-new windows of any kind to paint, make sure to prime the tops, bottoms, and sides of them. You can also buy new windows already primed, which I think is worth it.

Window and Door Frames

You are working against time with enamel. When you come back to join a spot that you painted much more than 20 minutes earlier, things can get sticky. The problem is feathering into paint that has already started to dry and become tacky. There is an easy order to trim work that keeps this drying factor from becoming a problem. In enamels, things will not look nice in places where you have fussed over paint that has started to dry. It won't look the same as the surrounding area. The trick is to have an entire section coated, with distinct ending points or edges, before you move on or take a break. To assure that things go smoothly and turn out well, paint in sections.

When brushing a window and the frame around it, you would start with the window itself. I discuss windows in detail in the section on double-hung windows. These types are the most complex, and a description of how they are done will leave you ready for any type of window.

For the trim around the window, like that around the door, you want to work from the top down, to avoid bumping or leaning on wood that you have just coated. Once the window itself is coated, begin with the top section of the frame. Apply paint from the window itself all the way to where the trim meets the wall. In rooms with stairs or balconies it is possible to see the tops of window frames, so get in the habit of coating them. Plus, it's good protection for the wood.

Coat the entire top piece of trim. You want to get the paint well into the corners at either end of this piece. Don't ever place a brushful of paint directly into a corner, however. This will leave too much there and it will run out and sag. Instead, get paint into corners when the bulk of that brushful has been applied more towards the middle of the trim piece. Stroke out the piece and lay it off. Then move on to the next part of the trim. When the sides and top of the window frame are laid off, you then finish by painting the window sill and any trim under it. Again, don't spend extra time at the junction between trim and wall, just make sure that the paint extends at least to this junction, then "dry brush" off any excess that remains on the wall. You will come through later and cut in this edge carefully with the wall color.

Door frames are painted in a similar order, but it isn't necessary to paint the door first, because it doesn't touch the frame anywhere. I usually paint the windows and their frames along with the door frames in one session, and roll and brush the doors themselves in another session. These are different operations, and you want to do the doors swiftly and move on, because the large surface area of a door gives off a lot of fumes, especially when using oil enamel.

It is easiest to reach all parts of a door frame with the door removed. If you are painting only one room, only half of the door frame will be painted. In this case the brushing order would be the top piece and then each side piece. Start at the caulk joint where trim meets wall, and carry the paint around to the door stop, one section of trim at a time. The door stop is the piece of trim in the middle of the casing that the door touches when closed. It is easy to make a clean, straight edge here, because the door stop stands off the rest of the casing and you can use the edge of it as the stopping place for your brush.

Stop several inches short of the floor on door frames, to avoid picking up dirt in your brush. You will coat these spots when you come around and hit the baseboards at the end of your enamel session.

When you are painting several rooms with the same color, you will paint both sides of the door frame. Remove the door for easy access and brush the top of the frame, then step through the doorway and hit the other side of the top piece, and blend the two together at the door stop. This way you stay ahead of the drying problem by quickly joining one side with the other. Next do both sides of one vertical, then the other, in the same way. Again, leave the last few inches at the floor for later, to keep your bucket and brush free of dirt and grit.

Overlapping enamel is easy if you don't wait too long. A firm pull of the brush over the surface that already has paint on it, in this case the door stop, evenly pulls out the slightly stickier paint and leaves it looking nice when it dries. Any place where you know you will be back to blend shortly, leave the brush strokes thin and even, free of globs and splotches. Then when you return to overlap at this spot the paint will lay off evenly and attractively.

Doors

Using a roller and brush in combination is a very efficient way to enamel doors. First set up your roller bucket as described in rolling. A thin foam roller cover is perfect for applying enamel and goes in the trash can when you are through. A three-inch brush works well here, because the approach is to get a section of the door rolled out uniformly and then to lay it off with the brush.

The easiest door to roll is, of course, the flat, one-surface kind. There are also doors with one or more panels, windows, etc., that work best when painted in a certain order. But for starters I will describe painting the single-surface door.

Remove the door knob and latch mechanism with a screwdriver. Blow the dust out of the holes, or vacuum it out. This hole-where-the-door-knob-used-to-be is the best place to hold onto a door when you are painting both sides and an unpainted spot to grab onto becomes scarce. I remove doors when I paint door-frames, because it is easier to reach the vertical sections, where the hinges are, when the door is off, plus it's faster. Popping the door off is quickly done using a hammer and screwdriver to tap the hinge pins out. I don't remove the hinges themselves, I paint around them. You may wish to tape off the hinges with masking tape if you feel uneasy about cutting around them by hand. Remember to remove the tape as soon as you are through, so that you can wipe off any paint that has crept behind the tape before it dries.

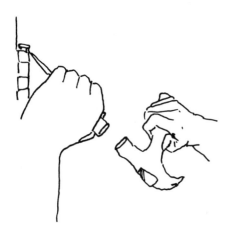

Popping a door off its hinges makes painting the frame quicker and easier.

I paint the door itself in place, because it is held in space perfectly by the hinges, not touching or leaning against anything as it dries. I might recommend removing a door and painting it in the garage if the door is over thick carpet and you fear you may get paint on it. When the door is over linoleum or wood floors, it's easiest to put down newspaper or a drop cloth and paint it in place.

When you dust off the door prior to painting, clean the top edge thoroughly, because your brush will reach around the top as you are painting the upper section and grab any dirt and grime that has built up there over the years.

With the thin foam roller you gently apply paint to both edges of the door. The roller gets 95 percent of the edge covered, and as you lay it off with a "dry" brush you paint up to the edge of the hinges. Next, notice that the roller has probably sent some paint around the corner as you rolled the edge and some substantial runs are proceeding down the face of the door at the edge. A dry brush will reduce these at this point with ease, yet will be difficult to remove if too much time goes by. Rollers always do this, unless you barely press down on the roller as you apply the paint. The door may already have large sags at the edges, and you can blame those on the previous painter. If it's a brand new door, well then, they're your sags.

When you are rolling the broad faces of the door, you need to watch out for the same problem. I always apply paint to the middle of the door with the full roller. Then I roll around the border with a some-what drier roller, to avoid sending paint around the corners to sag later if not brushed out. This is a technique that has worked very well for me over the years. In brushing or rolling, it is easier to pick up paint that you have stored on the surface that you are painting, than to reach back and dip in the bucket. On the door we are dis-cussing, I would dip the roller until full, then run the roller up the center of the door from about the height of the knob to the top of the door, pushing most of the paint out of the roller in this one stroke. One dip of these foam rollers is enough paint to fully coat an area about the size of half a door.

What this means is that I can get the paint from the bucket and store it in the middle of the door, while I use the "drier" roller to get the spots that are a hassle with a full roller. And, I save time spent chas-ing sags down the edges, since they are less likely to occur with the "dry" roller. The less paint there is in the roller, the less excess there is to creep around the edges of things.

The foam roller is used to move the paint around the region until it is uniformly covered. At this point there should be no dark spots; it should look like all one color. Tilt the roller at an angle and press the excess paint out of both ends onto the door, and give the upper half of the door a final roll, like the final touch in rolling walls. This section should now have a uniform orange-peel finish. This refers to a look that is not smooth but slightly dimpled throughout, hence the name. What you then do with your dry brush is to gently lay off the paint, a stroke at a time, starting with your brush in the lower unpainted area and running it smoothly up the door and off the top. Don't pass off the top of the door with too much spring in your bristles, or paint drops will splatter in all directions. Laying off strokes are gentle, with very little spring in the bristles.

Next, the lower section is dealt with in the same way. Overlap your upper section a bit as you roll to avoid thin spots, and lay off from the bottom upwards, gently pulling your brush away when you are well into the upper region, maybe six inches above the height of the door knob.

The first U.S. Patent for a paint formula included zinc oxide, potassium hydroxide, resin, milk, and linseed oil. It was issued in 1865.

Rolling and then brushing is the fastest way to get a door perfectly coated. The brush strokes will be even, since this quickness assures that you will be finished brushing before the paint starts to get sticky. The roller is used to apply the paint, the brush to cut in around the hinges and lay off the paint. Pass the brush gently over the hole from the door knob, or you will leave a large deposit there that will sag later. Wipe out excess paint with a rag before moving on.

Doors with panels are a little different. These require a bit more brushing time, and are painted in sections. Start at the top of the door and work your way down. On an older door with three panels, for example, you would first gently roll both edges. Check for sags. Next, I hit the boards that stand out towards me, that is, the perimeter and any others that divide the panels. Use the roller to get these boards coated, and brush some paint down the slope and an inch or two onto the recessed panel. This slope is usually a piece of milled wood that has some decorative profile. As usual, the last step is to lay off a section then proceed to the next.

Leave the paint on the panels thin and even, without globs and splotches, so you can overlap these spots neatly when you come back to them. I would leave the bottom horizontal until the very last, because drips will probably land on it as I work above. With all the boards except the bottom one laid off, what remains are the panels themselves, and these I would paint one at a time with the roller and brush. Having earlier brought the paint onto each panel an inch or so, my meeting place would be at the edge of each panel, at the "foot" of each decorative slope. There would be no need to place my brush on the vertical or horizontal boards, and I would simply lay off the panel to where it meets the trim. Last I would hit the bottom board, repeat on the other side of the door, and the door is done.

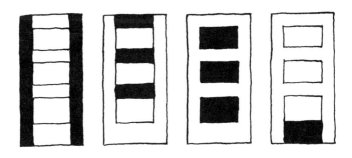

When the door is coated, remove your newspaper or drop cloth and leave the door in the fully open position to dry. Keep it from blowing shut with a wedge of wood under the door. If the door is over carpet, leave the newspaper in place until it dries. Better to remove a little stuck newspaper from the bottom of the door tomorrow than to find dried paint in the carpet.

Cabinets

Cabinets, book cases and counters are easy to paint with the roller/brush combination described in the section on painting doors. You apply paint with the roller and lay it off with the brush. I set up a five-gallon bucket with about half a quart of enamel in the bottom and use a thin foam roller.

For cabinets, I work the insides first. Starting at the top, I get paint on the back and top of the compartment with the roller. Then, with a full brush, I get paint distributed in the dry corners bordering the back and top. Next, I move the paint around with the brush until everything is wet. Finally, I wipe the brush on the edge of the bucket and then lay off these two sections, starting in the corners with my strokes. With the back and top of the compartment laid off, I repeat the process on the sides and the shelf of this first compartment. Care must be taken to lay off the front edge of a shelf. A dry roller applies paint to this edge perfectly, but when laying off I keep the bristles from reaching around and disturbing the shelf surface itself, which has already been laid off. Often it is a game of back and forth, laying off the front edge and then the shelf surface again, until I am satisfied that both surfaces are laid off nicely. I then continue on down the inside of the cabinet until all the compartments are coated and laid off.

This completes the inside of the cabinet. Next I attend to the "carcass." This is the actual term for the body of a cabinet, minus its doors and drawers. If this were a book case with no doors, finishing the piece would be a matter of coating the front and sides. With the roller and brush, this is achieved in no time.

Drawers should be removed and numbered with a pencil somewhere that won't show, so you know where each one goes when you are finished painting. They are usually not interchangeable. Also remove the handles and wash them while they're off. The drawers should be painted while they are out of the cabinet, and stood on a drop cloth to dry.

If the piece had doors on it, I would coat the "carcass," including the hinges if they have previously been painted. Then I am simply left with the cabinet doors, where the roller and brush once again are quite handy. The handles having been removed, I hold the door in place with one finger on the top or bottom as I brush and roll. This little spot gets a dab of paint once I have coated both sides. One side of a cabinet door is small enough to paint with one roller's worth of paint, and then I lay that side off all at once.

All built-in cabinets and shelves should be caulked where they meet the wall. Always carry the enamel at least to this junction, and leave the careful cutting in until you come back through with the wall color.

A mantle piece or counter-top is rolled and brushed in the same way. So is the wainscot, if you have an older house. The wainscot should be painted as you would a wall with enamel, only in this case the wall is only about waist-high. Work from a corner and don't stop in the middle of a section. Keep overlapping the enamel and only consider taking a break when you have reached a corner. Always leave the last several inches at the floor until the end of your enamel session, to keep your brush free of dirt and dust.

Baseboards

Baseboards should be the last thing that you enamel, so that any dust and hairs from the floor that foul your bucket and brush won't be carried up onto trim work that is more visible. Also, the bucket should contain a small amount of paint when you do the baseboards, because you will dispose of this paint due to the debris that you will pick up, and not return it to the paint can when you are through.

Baseboards are trickiest where carpet is present. Run a vacuum cleaner carefully along the carpet edge to remove as much loose dust as possible. A one-and-one-half inch brush is easiest to control when you are working near carpet. A paint shield is useful, available at your paint store. This is a tool that you can place over the carpet to keep paint off as you brush the baseboard. You must use care even with a paint shield, as excess paint builds up quickly and you can get it on the carpet anyway if you are not careful. Best to wipe the shield with a rag as you go. Any tool that keeps paint from getting where you don't want it is useful only if you are careful. Assuming that the carpet is safe and then getting sloppy with the brush will only get you into a mess. Paint mistakes on carpet clean pretty easily if you attend to them immediately, thinner for oil paints and water for latex. Keep a rag and some thinner at hand as you go, so you can catch errors as soon as they occur.

Keeping the brush out of the carpet is the hardest part here. The section on cutting in describes tricks on getting paint up to an edge effectively. Carry the paint up onto the wall a bit, at least covering the joint between wall and baseboard. You will come back later and cut in this joint neatly with the wall color. Use the width of the brush to lay off the coat and assure an even look, as described in the section on handling a brush.

Baseboards in a room with wood floors are much easier. Vacuum the borders all the way around the room after you have swept dust away from the walls. This leaves less dust to be kicked up as the paint is drying. You may wish to mask the floor with tape where it meets the baseboard, but be prepared to remove it as soon as you have painted to prevent paint from seeping behind the tape to dry. My technique is to skip the tape and carefully but boldly cut in against the floor by hand. Get the baseboard completely coated to where it meets the floor. Doing this sometimes results in a little paint getting on the floor. Wiping the paint off of the floor, but not disturbing the paint on the baseboard is easily achieved using a putty knife with a linen or cotton rag wrapped over the blade. Or, you can use a scraper to get in the corner and gently remove paint from the floor. This leaves a nice, clean line where the baseboard meets the floor. Whatever approach you use, just remember that paint mistakes are easiest to clean up when they happen, rather than when they are dry.

Of course, the best way to have that nice, clean edge is to paint the baseboard before it is installed, which applies to new construction but is rarely an option when painting existing baseboard. In many cases, if the floors are being refinished, the base-shoe of the baseboard is removed so the floor can be worked as close to the baseboards as possible. This is an opportunity to repaint the base-shoe, which is simply a piece of quarter-round wood sometimes fitted along the bottom of the baseboard itself. It is used to close the gaps that occur at the edge of floors. It is often put in place over linoleum to give the corner a finished look. If you are able to paint the base-shoe prior to installation, you won't have to cut in against the floor at all. Just prime, sand and paint it in a convenient spot where it can dry overnight. A couple of sawhorses in the garage is a perfect set-up. All of this also applies to the baseboard, of course, if it is being removed or replaced for any reason.

Once the base-shoe is pre-painted, the procedure is as follows: Nail it into place and set the nails, fill the holes with linseed putty, caulk the joint between base-shoe and baseboard, and let the caulk dry. Linseed putty is used here because it won't show through the enamel finish coat as a dull spot, because it is oil-based and doesn't need to be spot-primed. With your baseboard prepped, primed and ready to go, all that remains is to finish coat the baseboard itself, covering the caulked seams and putty-filled holes, but staying well away from the floor with the brush.

The sharpest look is always achieved when trim is pre-painted before it gets installed against a contrasting surface such as natural wood, counter-tops, tile, etc. One last detail—when you pre-paint the quarter-round base-shoe, the primer that you apply to the baseboard itself, if any, need only be brought to within a half-inch of the floor, because the base-shoe covers that much of the baseboard when installed. This depends on the size quarter-round you use for the base-shoe, half inch in this case.

Picture rails, crown molding, and decorative trim are more often found in older homes. These are simple to paint. When they are prepped and caulked, simply brush them out, with a small overlap onto the walls. If they are to be the same paint as the walls, you can do this as you are cutting in prior to rolling the walls. If you are using a different paint to accent such trim, brush it as you are doing the rest of the trim and leave a slight overlap for when you come back though to cut in the wall color.

Clean-Up

You may wish to use some rubber gloves when you clean brushes containing oil-based paint. You will also need three wide-mouth quart jars with lids, a gallon of thinner, a wire brush, some newspaper, and a clean one-gallon bucket.

Fill all three jars about two-thirds of the way with thinner, and write 1, 2, and 3 on the lids with a felt pen. These three jars of thinner can be used again and again, in order, to clean oil brushes. Jar #1 will become most loaded with the paint material. When it becomes overloaded, discard the contents and pour #2 into it, then #3 into #2 jar. After that, re-fill #3 with fresh thinner. You can clean brushes maybe 10 times before the contents of jar #1 will need to be discarded.

Using the paint brush, I wipe the excess paint out of the bucket that I used that day. I then set the bucket aside somewhere free of moisture to let the last bit of paint dry overnight. Next, I lay the paint brush between two pages of the newspaper and place the edge of my hand, like a karate chop, on top of the paper so that I am touching the metal part of the brush underneath. Then I press down with the edge of my hand and at the same time slowly pull the brush out from under it, using the handle. This will leave the bulk of the paint in the newspaper. Repeat this several times and every bit of paint you remove won't end up in your thinner.

Next, pour the thinner from container #1 into your clean bucket. Toss your brush in there and work the thinner up into the bristles. Then, the wire brush is used to remove built-up paint from the place where the bristles meet the metal. This is done by laying the brush on the edge of the bucket and firmly stroking away from you with the wire brush. Each stroke should begin on the metal and pass down the bristles and off the far end of the paint brush. Do this to both sides of the paint brush, and both edges. Built-up paint from that day will come loose and the quantity of paint that has accumulated in the upper part of the bristles will be greatly reduced.

Holding the brush by the handle in one hand, you next squeeze the bristles with the other, letting the thinner fall back into the bucket. This is the part where the rubber gloves keep the thinner off your hands. Using your hands to clean a brush is the only way to get all the paint out and insure that the brush can be re-used many times.

The cleaning process from here on is to dip and squeeze repeatedly. After a minute of this, return the contents of your bucket to container #1, and pour container #2 into the bucket. Wire brush once again, and then it's dip and squeeze, a few minutes in #2 thinner, then a few minutes in #3. By now, any remaining paint is easy to see. As you squeeze the paint brush it will streak out from the upper reaches of the bristles.

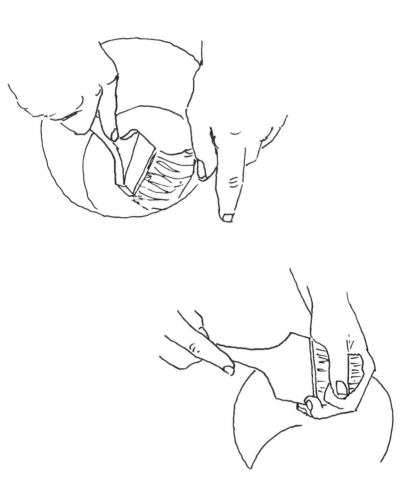

If this is your first time cleaning out brushes this way, watch how long you can spend in #3 thinner and still see paint streaking out of the upper bristles. Dried paint in quantity here renders a brush useless, because it gets rock hard, won't hold paint, and loses flexibility.

Spin out the brush between the different thinners by placing the handle between your palms and moving your hands in opposite directions. Hold the bristles above the level of the thinner but below the top of the bucket as you spin, or thinner will spray over you and the area in which you are cleaning. I clean my brushes outdoors or, if it's raining, on the garage floor over a drop cloth. When the brush looks good and clean in the upper bristles, give it one last spin, replace it in its jacket, and it is ready to go the next time.

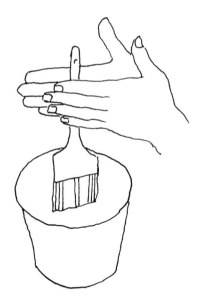

The same wire brush procedure applies to latex brushes, while the water you use is simply poured in a corner of the yard and replaced with fresh until the brush is clean. Better to pour water with paint in it in an out-of-the-way place in the yard, than to wash it all down the sink where it could build up and cause drainage problems. Or, do the major cleaning outdoors, and come inside to the sink to rinse the last bit of latex there, working a little hand soap into the bristles as the final cleaning step.

State and local environmental laws may not allow this. Ask at your paint dealer for laws that apply to where you live.

If you have been rolling oil-based paints, simply wrap a sheet of newspaper around the roller, pull it off the handle, and throw it away. You will want to run the brush around the inside of the 5 gallon bucket and remove the excess paint from it, as you did the smaller paint bucket. This allows the paint to dry so the bucket is ready to use the next day. I don't clean paint buckets out with thinner, because you go through thinner too quickly that way.

Cleaning out a latex roller bucket is another operation that I do in the yard. I select an out-of-the-way place where the garden hose reaches. I pull the roller a few inches off the handle so that it won't dry stuck in place. I then direct the hose at the side of the roller, and it gradually starts to spin. I reach around the five-gallon bucket when I do this, so that it shields me from the the paint and water that spins off the roller. One minute of rinsing the roller with the hose, directing it up and down the roller as it spins, will leave the roller clean for later use. Next, I rinse the inside of the bucket with a powerful spray from the hose, which removes all the latex that is still wet. I pour this out and then proceed to hose down the entire area, diluting the paint on the ground so that the lawn is still green when I am done.

A less messy way to clean a roller, and the only way if you have no yard to go crazy in as I do, is available at the paint store. It is a little gadget that spins the roller for you, so that the whole operation can be done within the confines of a five-gallon bucket. You pull the roller off the handle, slide it onto this tool, and then dunk it in the bucket, half-filled with water. Then you spin it out, above the level of the water but below the top of the bucket. After replacing the water a couple times for a cleaner rinse each time, this way works, too. It's far less messy, but not as much fun.

Again, find out the approved way to dispose of latex and rinse water where you live.

In World War Two, the U.S. developed a paste that would turn into camouflage paint when you added gasoline or water.

Paints and Colors

The big question for the do-it-yourself painter is whether to use latex or oil paint for the trim. We could argue the pros and cons for each, but the final point remains: Oil paints last on trim for years, while latex can't. Latex cannot take the wear on cabinets, drawer fronts, doors, or windows. Fumes are a valid objection people have to using oils, yet ventilation can reduce these considerably.

The choice is yours. If you feel better about latex, use it. Just remember that latex peels and chips much more readily than oil. Choosing latex may seem convenient today, but the price you pay is more frequent repainting down the road.

I don't expect everyone to share my enthusiasm for oil paints, and I will say that latex enamels are acceptable for the kitchen, bath, and laundry room walls. Again, oil will last longer, and withstand repeated washing and scrubbing long after latex has started to break down, but you can get away with latex semi-gloss for a couple of years on the walls. Also, remember to have mold preventive added to your paint for any room in the house that has a moisture problem.

The most important law of paint physics is that you cannot put latex enamel over a previous coat of oil enamel. It will not adhere properly. You must prime with a suitable primer, then apply the latex. Oil, on the other hand, can be applied directly to previous coats of oil or latex enamel, after you have sanded to reduce the gloss. Your paint dealer has details, and maybe even a product that can safely ignore this law. Find out about this, because after all your hard work on the trim, it deserves a durable finish coat.

When shopping, don't buy cheap paint. Go to a name brand paint store that you trust and buy quality paint. This will save you time and money now, because cheap paints often require two coats. Quality paint will also save you time and money later, because it will hold up well and need repainting far less frequently than cheaper products.

Name brand flat latex wall paint is the way to go in any room that you do not wish to have shiny walls.

All enamels, oil or latex, are formulated to have different degrees of shine, such as high gloss, semi-gloss, or low gloss. Using a lower gloss enamel makes minor blemishes less noticeable. Some people prefer the dull glow of a low gloss versus the "wetter" look of semi-gloss. Your paint dealer will show you samples of these different paints on request.

I personally prefer the look of low gloss enamel, and recommend it to my customers. It is more forgiving of surface imperfections because it doesn't catch the light as much as higher glosses do, and if you are painting over many decades of paint layers, that can really help. Low gloss paint also doesn't show your brush marks as much. If you combine careful preparation with a low gloss enamel finish, existing wood often looks like new when you are finished. These different gloss paints are available in oil or latex.

When estimating how much paint you will need, remember that colors that are kept in stock at the paint store can be returned if you don't open the can. So simply buy plenty, and return the rest. The rule of thumb is about 400 square feet per gallon. A measuring tape and calculator will give you an educated guess. Clerks at the paint store can help estimate how much paint you will need.

Custom colors, on the other hand, are not returnable. You should mix all the gallons of a custom color together in a five-gallon bucket before you start. This is because colors mixed by hand at the store don't always match exactly from can to can, like stock colors from the factory. Mixing them all together assures that all the paint for the job will be uniform. If you run short when using a custom color, the gallon that you pick up to finish the job may not match exactly, and this can lead to problems and wasted time. So buying a little extra custom paint, even though you can't return it, is better than buying too little.

A gallon goes a long way when you are painting trim. For quarts, a rough rule of thumb is that one quart covers both sides of three doors with ease, while four doors is cutting it close.

Latex wall paints arrived in 1948.
1957 saw the arrival of exterior latex
house paint, and in 1970 latex
semi-gloss became available.

Choosing colors is fun, and color plays an important role in how a room "feels." Books on color and color psychology make interesting reading. One rule of thumb is that lighter colors make a room seem larger, and darker colors make it seem smaller. For example, a bright white ceiling will seem higher than a darker one, so a light ceiling will make the room seem brighter and more airy. Or, a large room can be made to seem more cozy with dark wall colors. A common practice is to paint the ceiling a nice, bright white color to multiply the light, and then paint the walls a creamy or tan off-white color.

Paint stores carry dozens of ready-mixed or "stock" colors, plus hundreds of custom colors that can be mixed for you on the spot. When deciding on colors, your paint dealer will have some useful suggestions.

Colors don't always look the same on the wall as they do on the little samples at the paint store. The reflected color of the carpet or other furnishings at home can make the appearance change even more. What I do is narrow down the choice to two or three, and then buy a quart of each. Then I apply a large test patch of each color to the walls in different parts of the room, say 4x4 feet for each test patch. This way you can choose a color based on how it actually looks in the room, and you will know in advance that the color is what you want.

The ability of a particular color to cover in one coat has a lot to do with the type and amount of pigments used to mix that color. For example, a particular off-white might require two coats to fully cover, while a different off-white might easily do the job in one coat. It is quicker and more pleasant to paint with a color that covers very well than to use a color that barely hides what's underneath, and of course having to use two coats means more time and more money spent on paint.

Discuss the points raised in this section with the paint dealer and you should be ready for smooth sailing when you finish coat.

One last point—environmental laws vary from region to region, and you should know about these when you paint. Paint dealers know all about them, so learn from them.

Varnish and Stain

Interior varnish comes in four grades: high gloss, semi-gloss, low gloss, and flat. You can have the exact appearance you desire by choosing from this range. Higher gloss varnishes are runnier than those with less shine. This is because the particles in gloss varnish are finer, which is what gives the product more shine. This also makes them more prone to run and sag.

Any varnish is trickier to handle than paint, because it will run and sag if you apply it too thickly. You need to check back over your work as you varnish, to make sure you have not left these kinds of mistakes.

For the first coat on raw wood, it is best to add some thinner to your varnish, so that it penetrates the wood and locks in better. The next coat can be applied full strength, after a light sand with 220 grit and a thorough wipe-down with a tack cloth, to remove dirt and dust.

Any time you use a finish that will allow the appearance of the wood to show through, it is smart to first do a test on a scrap piece of the same kind of wood. The reason for this is that once you have applied a coat to raw wood, the stain or varnish passes into the pores, and is very difficult to remove if you don't like the effect.

This differs from painting a surface, because with paint there is no question about the final appearance. Since paints are opaque, the color is uniform and the results are the same no matter what type of surface you paint. There are exceptions to this, such as oak, mahogany, and other hardwoods. The pores of some of these woods are large, and hardwoods will not turn out glass-smooth, as fir and pine do when painted. As a general rule, therefore, hardwoods usually receive a clear finish, while the softer woods are usually painted.

Apply varnish with a quality oil brush, and clean up with thinner. Do not putty holes in the trim until after you have varnished. Colored putty is available to match all the different colors of wood. Remember, wood is very absorbent, and if you putty first, the varnish will not penetrate the same around the holes as elsewhere, and an uneven finished look will result. This mistake will look even worse if you are staining the wood, so be sure to putty last.

Applying stain is pretty messy. Use plenty of floor or carpet protection, and accept the fact that you will need to come back and brush the wall color up to the edge of the trim you have stained. Stain is about as thin as water, and a brush doesn't work very well. A piece of rag can be used, and you can force the stain into corners pretty well with it. Get a section wet, then wipe it one last time to remove excess. Before you take a break,check any surfaces you have stained to make sure that they don't have streaks. If the surface is not satisfactory, a clean rag with a little thinner can be used to carefully rub the area until it looks uniform.

A "stain mitten" is a good idea if you plan to stain large surfaces such as doors. This is a disposable mitten that covers your hand, and you dip it directly into the stain, then rub out the surface with it. It is a fun tool for this kind of job, and it works.

I would suggest three coats of varnish as a minimum, or two coats of stain followed by two coats of varnish, if you intend to change the color of the wood. Read the label for the manufacturer's recommendations.

Oriental laquer and shellac from India began to appear in Europe in the 1600's. A European monk left us a formula for varnish that he wrote down in the 1100's.

Ladders

A six-foot step ladder will take care of most interior painting situations. If you have a need to reach higher, you can rent or borrow a taller step ladder, or you can use an extension ladder, if you own one. Even with ceilings over 10 feet high, you will only need a tall ladder when you brush the edges of the ceiling. The rolling can usually be accomplished from the floor, using your extension handle.

Several tips will make your ladder experiences safe and worry-free. The most important thing when using a step ladder is to be sure that all four feet are resting squarely on the floor. To check this, I make sure that both of the cross-braces are fully locked in place. (These are the pieces that fold in half when you open or close a step ladder.) Next, I always climb onto the first step and pull the ladder towards me a bit. This causes the two far legs of the ladder to lift off the floor, and they will usually land in a spot that levels the ladder. Check this once or twice, because if the step ladder is not solidly set on all fours, it can buckle and jump out from under you, especially if you are on the upper steps.

Indoors, an extension ladder will stand safely on the floor. Just make sure that you use caution if placing the ladder on slick floors or tile. Secure the ladder to something structural with a section of rope if there is any doubt in your mind that the ladder might slip.

If you have a ceiling that is so high that you are using an extension ladder, you can use a thick wire hanger to hook and unhook your paint bucket from an upper rung as you work. Always bring the paint bucket down with you before you move the ladder, and keep less than an inch of paint in your bucket. I always make sure that a ladder is safe before I climb it, yet I still move carefully, because dropping a bucket with paint in it could splatter paint over a lot of expensive furnishings that are far outside the immediate work area.

The Romans and Italians developed the art of making frescos. This technique involves putting pigment in wet plaster so that the color locks into the wall when the plaster dries.

Materials Check List

First things first

Old, loose-fitting shirt and pants
Cap or bandanna
Work shoes
Eye protection and dust mask
Patience and a sense of humor

Scraping

Scraper handle and two blades
Metal file
Scrap piece of 2x4
One-and-one-half-inch putty knife
Three-inch putty knife

Sanding

Sheets of 100, 120, and 150 grit
    sandpaper
Medium-coarse steel wool
Sanding pole with detachable sand-
    ing pad
Dust mask and eye protection
Sanding machines (optional)

Cleaning

TSP
Wash bucket
Sponge mop
Sponge
Rags
Bleach
Paint thinner

Caulking

Latex caulk with silicone
Caulk gun
Several 16d finish nails
Blade to cut tip of caulk tube
Rags
Clean one gallon bucket

Filling

Hammer
Nail set
Light-weight filler
Linseed filler
Two-part auto body filler
One-and-one-half-inch putty knife
Three-inch putty knife
Non-porous surface for mixing auto
    body filler
Single-edge razors to clean putty
    knives

Brushing

One-and-one-half-inch oil brush
Two- or three-inch oil brush
One-and-one-half-inch latex brush
Two- or three-inch latex brush
Two plastic one-gallon buckets

Rolling

Roller handle
Roller cover for latex
Roller cover for oil
Roller extension handle
Two plastic five-gallon buckets
Roller screen for inside five-gallon
    bucket

Protection

Two-inch wide masking tape
Newspaper
Minimum 8x8-foot drop cloth
Minimum 3x8-foot drop cloth
Old sheets
Rags

Paints

Primer
Finish paints
Paint additives
Paint thinner

Clean-up

Single-edge razors to clean paint
    from glass
Three clean quart jars
Plastic one-gallon bucket
Wire brush
Newspaper
Rubber gloves
Spinner device (optional)
Rags

Step-By-Step Quick

Steps to prepare and paint a room with flat latex ceiling and walls, and gloss enamel trim:

1. Prep ceiling and walls.
2. Prep all woodwork.
3. Brush and roll ceiling and walls. This will be two separate steps if ceiling and walls are a different color. Do not brush wall paint up to the edge of the trim, leave this step for last.
4. Brush woodwork with gloss enamel, leaving sections at floor level for last. Allow to dry overnight.
5. Brush the wall color up to the trim.

Steps to prepare and paint a room to receive gloss enamel throughout, such as kitchen, bath, and laundry rooms:

1. Prep ceilings and walls.
2. Prep woodwork.
3. If you are using the same color throughout, and you are using oil, brush woodwork, then brush and roll ceilings, walls, and doors. I suggest this order so that you are exposed to the least fumes. Brushing the enamel puts out far less fumes than when you start rolling walls and ceilings with it, so I leave the broad surfaces until last. Latex fumes are not a problem.
4. If you are using a different color on the trim than on the walls, brush all the trim, then allow to dry overnight. The next day, cut in the entire room with the second color and brush and roll the ceiling and walls.

Reference Guide

Here are the steps for specific surfaces in the house:

Steps to prepare and paint existing flat latex ceilings and walls:

1. Broom away dust and spider webs.
2. Fill holes.
3. Caulk cracks.
4. Cut in corners with brush, then roll. This will be two separate steps if the ceiling and walls are a different color.
5. Leave brushing the wall color up to the trim until the trim has been completed.

New flat latex ceilings and walls are the same procedure as existing ones, but with two coats. Ask your paint dealer if their product is designed for two coats of wall paint or if a special primer is recommended. A light pole sanding between coats using 120 grit may be necessary if the surface was not carefully finished by the texturing worker. Wall defects show more clearly after a coat of paint has been applied.

Steps to prepare and paint existing gloss enamel walls:

1. Wash with TSP.
2. Fill holes.
3. Sand lightly with pole sander using 120 grit.
4. Caulk cracks.
5. Spot prime all patched holes, exposed wood or plaster, etc.
6. Brush and roll gloss enamel.

Steps to prepare and paint new gloss enamel walls:

1. All texturing work must be "painter ready." This means the surfaces are straight, uniform, and attractive, be it textured or smooth wall.
2. Fill holes.
3. Broom off dust, use dust mask.
4. Gently sweep or vacuum floor.
5. Brush and roll PVA primer.
6. Lightly pole sand, using 120 grit. If any high spots have been sanded down, and the primer has been sanded away in these areas, prime these exposed spots with PVA.
7. Caulk any cracks.
8. Brush and roll enamel.

Steps to prepare and paint existing wood trim, such as doors, windows, cabinets, and baseboards:

1. Set nail heads.
2. Scrape off all loose paint.
3. Sand carefully with 120 grit or finer.
4. Fill all holes, leave flush and sand lightly when filler hardens, using 120 grit.
5. Dust off all trim surfaces and those nearby. Make sure that the trim you intend to enamel is clean.
6. Spot prime all exposed wood, patches, and filled holes. Check drying time on label.
7. Spray any knots that have yellowed and are showing through with spray shellac. Check drying time on label.
8. Caulk all cracks. Check drying time on label.
9. Brush your trim with gloss enamel, and allow it to dry overnight.

Remember, when repainting gloss enamel trim, oil will grip a previous coat of either oil or latex, while latex will only bind properly to a previous coat of latex.

Steps to prepare and paint new wood:

1. Set nail holes.
2. Fill holes, leave flush and sand lightly when filler hardens, using 120 grit.
3. Dust off all trim surfaces and those nearby. Make sure that the trim you intend to prime is clean.
4. Spray all knots with spray shellac. Also spray any ink marks on the wood, like stamped words, numbers, etc. Check drying time on label.
5. Prime the wood; oil is best. Check drying time on label.
6. Sand with 120 grit or finer sandpaper. Use medium coarse steel wool on complex trim.
7. Dust off surfaces carefully.
8. Caulk all cracks. Check drying time on label.
9. Brush your trim with gloss enamel, and allow it to dry overnight.

For more beauty and protection, you may prime a second time and lightly sand with 120 grit or finer, between steps 7 and 8.

Steps to prepare and paint varnished or stained wood:

1. Set all nail heads.
2. Fill all holes, leave flush, then sand lightly when filler hardens.
3. Sand the trim carefully with 120 grit or finer.
4. Dust off all the trim and surfaces nearby, and make sure all the wood you intend to prime is clean.
5. Spray all knots with spray shellac, prime all the wood—oil is best. Check drying times on labels.
6. Lightly sand as necessary.
7. Dust off carefully.
8. Caulk all the cracks in the trim. Check drying time on label.
9. Brush your trim with gloss enamel, and allow it to dry overnight.

For more beauty and protection, you may prime a second time and lightly sand with 120 grit or finer, between steps 7 and 8.

Index

About This Book

This book was set in Century Old Style by Metro Typography, Santa Cruz, California
The book was printed by Watsonville Press, Watsonville, California